VALUE BIOGRAPHIES

KINDNESS
The Story of FRED ROGERS

IB LARSEN

childsworld.com

Published by The Child's World®
800-599-READ · www.childsworld.com

Copyright © 2026 by The Child's World®
All rights reserved. No part of this book may be reproduced or utilized in any form or by any means without written permission from the publisher.

Photography Credits
Photographs ©: Gene J. Puskar/AP Images, cover, 1, 7, 12, 13 (top), 15, 16, 18; Focus Features/Entertainment Pictures/Alamy, 5; Bettmann/Getty Images, 6; Shutterstock Images, 8–9, 13 (bottom); Noam Galai/Getty Images for Nantucket Film Festival/Getty Images Entertainment/Getty Images, 10; Red Line Editorial, 19; Family Communications Inc./Getty Images Entertainment/Getty Images, 20; Design element from Gene J. Puskar/AP Images

ISBN Information
9781503871229 (Reinforced Library Binding)
9781503872585 (Portable Document Format)
9781503873827 (Online Multi-user eBook)
9781503875067 (Electronic Publication)

LCCN 2024950383

Printed in the United States of America

Ib Larsen is a writer and an editorial assistant living in Saint Paul, Minnesota. He holds a bachelor's degree in English and mathematics. He is the author of several nonfiction books for young readers.

TABLE OF CONTENTS

CHAPTER 1

A SAVIOR OF PUBLIC TELEVISION 4

CHAPTER 2

THE VALUE OF KINDNESS 8

CHAPTER 3

BEING KIND TO ALL 14

Wonder More . . . 21
Fast Facts . . . 22
Act of Kindness . . . 22
Glossary . . . 23
Find Out More . . . 24
Index . . . 24

A SAVIOR OF PUBLIC TELEVISION

It was May 1, 1969. US **senators** were discussing how much money the government should spend on the Public Broadcasting Service (PBS). This is a public television (TV) network. Public TV is TV that does not intend to make money. Instead, it aims to educate its viewers. The government had given money to PBS in the past. But now senators were talking about reducing the money. That could cause some public TV shows to end.

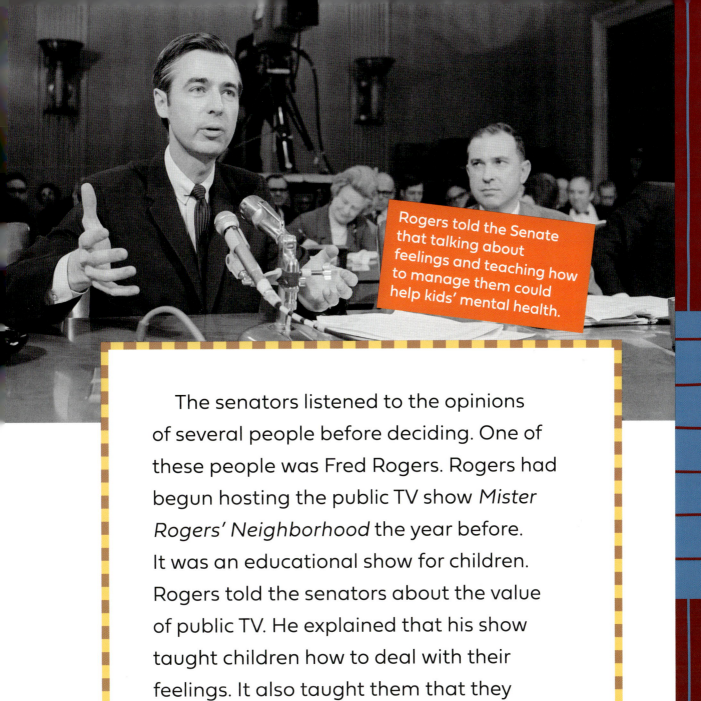

Rogers told the Senate that talking about feelings and teaching how to manage them could help kids' mental health.

The senators listened to the opinions of several people before deciding. One of these people was Fred Rogers. Rogers had begun hosting the public TV show *Mister Rogers' Neighborhood* the year before. It was an educational show for children. Rogers told the senators about the value of public TV. He explained that his show taught children how to deal with their feelings. It also taught them that they deserve kindness. Rogers argued that his young viewers may not hear those valuable messages without public TV.

Rogers was beloved by generations of children.

Rogers finished speaking. He had made his case well. One senator said that Rogers's speech had given him goose bumps. Then he said that they would not reduce money given to PBS.

Rogers appeared as a gentle, patient man on his show. Many young viewers appreciated the way he spoke to them. Rogers made them feel respected. He talked about issues children commonly face. And parents liked his show because of its educational content.

One subject Rogers often taught his viewers about was kindness. Kindness is when a person shows helpful concern for other people. Being kind has a lot of good effects on the world. Showing kindness to one person can cause that person to be kind to others. Being kind can also make a person feel as if they belong within a **community**.

I was a minister of the United Presbyterian Church.

CHAPTER 2

THE VALUE OF KINDNESS

Fred Rogers was born on March 20, 1928. He grew up in Latrobe, Pennsylvania. Rogers studied music composition in college. He later decided to work on children's TV shows. He worked on other people's shows at first. But then he had the chance to host his own show. This led to *Mister Rogers' Neighborhood*. His show aired on public TV from 1968 to 2001.

Kindness was a common theme on Rogers's show. It is a value shared by many people. Rogers was kind even when he did not have to be. He tried to help people feel valued.

Rogers studied at Rollins College in Winter Park, Florida. A sculpture honoring Rogers can be found on the Rollins campus.

François Clemmons is a singer, writer, and actor.

FRANÇOIS CLEMMONS

Officer Clemmons was played by François Clemmons, a gay actor. Gay people were not treated kindly in the 1960s and 1970s. Clemmons's being gay could have threatened the popularity of *Mister Rogers' Neighborhood*. Clemmons and Rogers agreed that Clemmons would keep it a secret. Today, many people in the United States are kinder to gay people. But gay people continue to face unkindness for who they are.

Rogers showed kindness in an episode of his show that aired on May 9, 1969. It was a hot day in this episode. Rogers had his feet in a pool to cool off. He invited a character called Officer Clemmons to join him. It was kind of Rogers to share the water with Officer Clemmons. But there was a deeper kindness to this act as well.

At this time in US history, many public swimming pools were **segregated**. Black people were not allowed to swim with white people. A law in 1964 had made segregation illegal. But some pools were still segregated in 1969. Many people were upset with this, including Rogers. He decided to take a stand on this issue. He did this by sharing his pool with Officer Clemmons, who was Black.

Rogers used many puppets on his show. They lived in the Neighborhood of Make-Believe. Rogers sent a trolley through a tunnel to bring viewers to and from the Neighborhood.

This act was kind to Rogers's Black viewers. Rogers showed these viewers respect that many other white people did not. Rogers was also being kind to the show's white viewers. Rogers taught these viewers that people of all races deserve the same respect. People continue to be inspired by Rogers's act of kindness.

IN HIS WORDS

In 2002, Rogers gave a speech to the graduating class of students at Dartmouth College. He said:

"What matters in this life is more than winning for ourselves. What really matters is helping others win, too. Even if it means slowing down and changing our course now and then."

Source: Dartmouth College, "Revisiting Fred Rogers' 2002 Commencement Address," *Dartmouth*, March 27, 2018. http://home.dartmouth.edu.

CHAPTER 3

BEING KIND TO ALL

Rogers took many opportunities to show kindness to the viewers of his show. He often read letters that viewers sent him. Rogers once received a letter from a young viewer named Katie. Katie was blind. But she liked to listen to *Mister Rogers' Neighborhood*.

Katie had a special request for Rogers. Rogers kept some fish in a tank on the set of *Mister Rogers' Neighborhood*. But he did not always say when he was feeding them.

Rogers began every episode by changing from traditional work clothes into a sweater and sneakers while singing a song. He did this to help viewers feel comfortable and safe.

After receiving a concerned letter from a blind fan, Rogers began saying when he was feeding his fish.

This was fine for Rogers's viewers who could see. But Katie worried about whether Rogers's fish were getting fed. She asked him to say something out loud whenever he fed his fish. After Rogers read her letter, he tried to remember to say that he was feeding the fish.

Rogers showed kindness to Katie with this act. He wanted to include her and his other blind fans. So he changed how he behaved on his show. People with unique needs are sometimes left out. **Accommodating** them is a way to reverse this. It is a show of kindness.

Rogers showed kindness to people when he was not on TV, too. Once, Rogers was going to have dinner with a TV **executive**. A **limousine** had been hired to take Rogers to the executive's home. The driver of the limousine was named Billy. Usually a limousine's driver is separated from the passenger. But Rogers rode in the front seat with Billy after the dinner. Rogers asked if he could meet Billy's family. Billy said yes. Rogers entertained Billy's family at their home by playing the piano.

I loved music. I wrote all of the music for *Mister Rogers' Neighborhood*.

MISTER ROGERS' WORLD

Latrobe, PA: Rogers's birthplace
Winter Park, FL: Where Rogers went to college
Pittsburgh, PA: Home of the set for *Mister Rogers' Neighborhood*
Toronto, Canada: Home of the set for *Misterogers*, an early version of *Mister Rogers' Neighborhood*
Washington, DC: Where Rogers defended PBS to senators

Rogers's attention was probably on the important TV executive that night. But he did not forget to be kind to his driver. He did not have much to gain by being kind to Billy. But he did it anyway. Rogers showed with this act that he believed all people deserve kindness.

Rogers died on February 27, 2003. Many people continue to watch old episodes of *Mister Rogers' Neighborhood*.

Rogers's legacy of kindness lives on.

Rogers's **legacy** is marked by his dedication to educating children and spreading kindness. The world is not always a kind place. But Rogers said that even in scary times, there are helpers nearby who are trying to be kind.

WONDER MORE

Wondering About New Information
How much did you know about kindness and Fred Rogers before reading this book? What new information did you learn? Write down three new facts that this book taught you. Was the new information surprising? Why or why not?

Wondering How It Matters
What is one way that kindness relates to your life? Can you think of a time when somebody showed you kindness? How do you think kindness relates to other kids' lives?

Wondering Why
Being kind sometimes requires thinking of other people's needs before thinking of your own. Why should people be kind even when they may not directly gain anything from it?

Ways to Keep Wondering
Kindness is a complex topic. After reading this book, what questions do you have about kindness? What can you do to learn more about being kind?

FAST FACTS

- Kindness is when a person shows helpful concern for others. Being kind has many benefits for people.

- Fred Rogers hosted an educational public TV show called *Mister Rogers' Neighborhood*.

- Rogers showed kindness to his viewers on many occasions. He also showed kindness to people in his life off screen.

- Rogers died on February 27, 2003. People remember him for his efforts to educate children and spread kindness.

ACT OF KINDNESS

1. Think about someone in your life to whom you could be kind. It could be a parent, a friend, or someone else.

2. Write down one kind thing you could do for that person. For example, you could tell them why you are grateful for them. Or you could give them a small gift.

3. Carry out that act of kindness. How did your act of kindness seem to make the other person feel? How did it make you feel?

GLOSSARY

accommodating (uh-KOMM-uh-day-ting) Accommodating someone means providing them with what they need. Accommodating people's unique needs is one way to be kind.

community (kuh-MYOO-nih-tee) A community is a group of people who have something in common. Kindness can make a person feel as if they belong within a community.

executive (egg-ZEK-yoo-tiv) An executive is a person in a leadership role within an organization. Rogers once dined at the home of a TV executive.

legacy (LEG-uh-see) A person's legacy is how they are seen by others after the person dies. Rogers's legacy is one of kindness and education.

limousine (lih-muh-ZEEN) A limousine is a large vehicle with a passenger area that is separated from the driver area. Rogers was once driven in a limousine by a driver named Billy.

segregated (SEH-gruh-gay-tid) A space is segregated if different groups of people are forced to be separated from each other within it. Many swimming pools in the 1960s were segregated by race.

senators (SEN-uh-turz) Senators are elected members of the US government who help make laws. Rogers gave a speech to senators about the value of public TV.

FIND OUT MORE

In the Library

Krekelberg, Alyssa. *Doing the Right Thing: Making Responsible Decisions*. Parker, CO: The Child's World, 2021.

Meltzer, Brad. *I Am Mister Rogers*. New York, NY: Rocky Pond Books, 2023.

Rudd, Maggie C. *Sometimes It's Hard to Be Nice*. Chicago, IL: Albert Whitman & Company, 2021.

On the Web

Visit our website for links about kindness and Fred Rogers:

childsworld.com/links

Note to Parents, Caregivers, Teachers, and Librarians: We routinely verify our web links to make sure they are safe and active sites. So encourage your readers to check them out!

INDEX

accommodation, 14–17

Billy (driver), 18–19

Clemmons, François, 10, 11–12
college, 8, 13, 19
community, 7, 11–12, 17, 18–19

fish, 14–17

helping, 7, 8, 13, 14–17, 20

Katie (fan), 14–17

Pennsylvania, 8, 19
public TV, 4–6, 8, 19

respect, 7, 11–12, 14–17, 19

segregation, 11
senators, 4–6